D0021493

DAVE BARRY'S
Gift Guide
to End All Gift Guides

DAVE BARRY'S
Gift Guide
to End All Gift Guides

Dave Barry

Crown Publishers, Inc.
New York

Photographs on pages 15–53, 57, 64–74, 89–91 by Douglas Karn and Bill Wax; Pages 55, 59, 60, 77–87, 93–126 copyright © 1994 by *The Miami Herald*

Published by Crown Publishers, Inc., 201 East 50th Street, New York, New York 10022. Member of the Crown Publishing Group.
Random House, Inc., New York, Toronto, London, Sydney, Auckland

Material in this book first appeared in the *Miami Herald*

CROWN is a trademark of Crown Publishers, Inc.

Manufactured in the United States of America

Library of Congress Cataloging-in-Publication Data
Barry, Dave.
(Gift guide to end all gift guides)
Dave Barry's gift guide to end all gift guides/Dave Barry—
1st ed.
p. cm.
1. Gifts—Humor. I. Title
PN6162.B297 1994
818' . 5407—dc20   94-19235
CIP

ISBN 0-517-79952-9
10 9 8 7 6 5 4 3 2 1

First Edition

*This book is dedicated to the retail sector,
without which we would not know the true meaning
of the holiday season.*

INTRODUCTION

When I was a small boy, gift shopping was simple, because I had very few people to buy gifts for, and once I found a gift that worked, I stuck with it, year after year. For example, I always gave my father a belt. I got it at the five-and-ten-cent store for about a dollar. It was made from what appeared to be genuine hand-tooled cardboard. I doubt that my father ever wore any of these belts, because if the humidity got over 50 percent they would dissolve. But it never occurred to me to wonder whether my father needed a belt; all I knew was that belts were in my price range, and he always said thank you.

I always gave my mother a little bottle of toilet water, which also cost about a dollar. At first I believed that this was water from an actual *toilet*, and I had no idea what she was supposed to do with it. But it came in a nice bottle, and it was also in my price range, and my mother always acted thrilled, holding the bottle up for general admiration.

"Look what Davey got me!" she'd exclaim, in a voice containing no hint of the fact that this was the fourth consecutive Christmas she'd received it. "Toilet water!"

I usually made Christmas gifts for my sister. One year I made her a paperweight by getting some clay and letting it harden, thereby forming a hardened lump of clay.

"What is this?" she asked.

"A paperweight," I said.

"Thank you," she said, which I now realize was very gracious of her. It was not as if the lack of a good paperweight had left a gaping hole in her life.

Another year I made her a bookmark. It looked very much like an ordinary strip of construction paper, but the trained eye could tell it was a bookmark, because on it were written, in crayon, the words BOOK MARK. I am sure she couldn't wait to finish opening her other presents so she could race to her room and mark some books.

The point is, gift-giving was simple for me then. As you have no doubt noticed, the older you get, and the more obligations you develop, the more complex the gift-giving becomes. This is especially true if you have children on your gift list. Meeting the gift needs of a single modern child requires an effort of roughly the same magnitude as the Normandy Invasion.

You parents know what I'm talking about. You know what it means to race from store to store, looking desperately for the Number-One Item on your eight-year-old son's wish list, namely the Official NASA Model Junior Space Shuttle, which takes seventeen years to assemble and leaks real hydrogen. You know what it means to get into a semiviolent dispute with another parent over who gets to purchase the only remaining model of the heavily advertised hot new toy concept Baby Fester Face ("The Doll with Open Sores That Really Run!"), which your five-year-old daughter has informed you she absolutely MUST have this year, and if she doesn't get it, she's going to put her own self up for adoption.

But at least children know what they want. It's much harder to decide what to get for grown-ups, who almost never know what they want, which is why we generally wind up giving them stupid things. For example, men are always getting cologne. I have never, in my whole life, heard a man express even the slightest interest in cologne. But most of us have numerous bottles of it, dating back to the Johnson administration.

What do men *really* want? I am generalizing here, of course, but I'd say that what men really want is to be left alone at key moments. For example, if you're in a relationship with a man, and you have decided, after much thought, that the two of you need to have a long, probing conversation in which you both sincerely try to understand each other's innermost feelings, then the man would consider it a wonderful gift if you would NOT announce your decision during an important televised football game (defined as "any televised football game").

Another great gift for a guy would be to tell him that you took the car in and had the oil changed AND the tires rotated.

But usually what we get is cologne.

What women really want, of course, is for men to share their innermost feelings. So what most men give them is appliances. I was guilty of this for many years, until I realized that although my wife could *appreciate* a fine appliance, she couldn't really *cherish* it. You never see scenes like this in the movies:

BRAD: Well, Dorothy, I'm off to the war.

DOROTHY: Oh, Brad, please be careful!

BRAD: I shall, Dorothy. But just in case I don't come back, I want you to have this.

DOROTHY (*tears of happiness streaming down her face*): Oh, Brad! It's a General Electric Coffee Maker with 12-Cup Capacity *and* Auto-Timer Function!

I have gradually learned that, as a rule, women prefer romantic items, which technically can be defined as "items that are small but cost a lot and do not have plugs," such as jewelry. The ultimate romantic gift for a woman would be a *single molecule* of some extremely expensive substance in a tiny cherishable box.

But you'll probably get her a Water Pik, you dork.

And here's an even bigger problem: What kind of gift do you get for people you don't really even want to give gifts to? I'm talking about all the neighbors and relatives and business associates who always give *you* something, leaving you with no choice but to give them a Retaliation Gift. But what? This is the question that pushes shoppers to the brink of insanity. This is what drives them to purchase ludicrous items that appear only during the holiday season and have no conceivable function in human society other than to be gifts, such as electronic dental-floss reconditioners, or soap shaped like fruit, or McDonald's gift certificates ("Oh, Brad! French fries!").

Well, if there's one goal that we have here, aside from never working on weekends, it's that we want to do everything we can to make your life easier. That's why we went to so much trouble to prepare *Dave Barry's Gift Guide to End All Gift Guides*.

The effort began when we assembled our team of Gift Guide Buyers, gave each one an unlimited expense account, and sent them off to scour the globe in search of the ultimate in unique and tasteful gift concepts. We have learned to "expect the unexpected" from our highly trained shopping professionals, but even WE were amazed when, six months later, none of them returned. We have NO idea where they are now, although the State Department has notified us that at one point they threw a party that resulted in considerable damage to Belgium.

Nevertheless, we want to stress that every item meets our Gift Guide Standards of Quality Excellence, which means:

1. THESE ARE REAL ITEMS THAT YOU CAN ACTUALLY BUY. We swear we did not make any of them up, *not even the Nose Spreader*.

2. THESE ITEMS HAVE PASSED OUR RIGOROUS INSPECTION PROGRAM. Before we include any item in the Gift Guide, we always inspect it carefully to see if maybe it's something that we might actually want to take home. So far, we never have.

3. THESE ITEMS ARE BACKED BY OUR EXCLUSIVE 100 PERCENT BUYER PROTECTION PLAN. If you purchase

a Gift Guide item, and for any reason you are dissatisfied, you may obtain a full cash refund merely by sending the item to us, along with your receipt and a color photograph of Tipper Gore naked.

Ha ha! We are just kidding, of course. Black and white is fine.

4. IT HAD TO BE SOMETHING THAT WE REMEMBERED TO ORDER IN TIME TO PUT IT IN THE GIFT GUIDE.

5. IT HAD TO BE CHEAP ENOUGH SO THAT THE LONG-SUFFERING OFFICE MANAGER AND BUDGET PERSON WOULD NOT LOOK AT THE BILL AND THEN TRY TO KILL US WITH A LETTER OPENER.

6. IT HAD TO ACHIEVE A LEVEL OF TASTELESSNESS SUCH THAT THE AVERAGE PERSON COULD NOT LOOK AT IT AND EAT AT THE SAME TIME.

We believe that the following items fill the bill. Of course we're not saying that you have to buy *exactly* these items. We're only saying that if you give gifts *like* these, then people will be far less likely to want to exchange gifts with you in the future.

We have also asked you, our readers, to suggest items for the Gift Guide. And we are glad we did. Because your suggestions proved that our suspicions were true: We ARE out of touch with your standards of decency. You don't HAVE any standards of decency. Some of your gift ideas, in terms of tastefulness, made Owl Vomit look like Waterford crystal.

Anyway, we're grateful to all of you who sent in ideas. Our only complaint is that many of you suggested gifts that do not actually exist. For example, Greg Blarr of Kenmore, New York, suggested "a combination enema and hide-a-key ($9.95; coated, $15.95)." No doubt many of us have often wished that there *were* such a product, but unfortunately there is not, and so we were forced to omit it from the Gift Guide. Our policy is to include only real items that you, the shopper, could actually purchase if you wanted to, probably as the result of a brain malfunction.

We also want to stress that we never put ANY item into the Gift Guide until it has been subjected to our strict testing procedures. So we feel confident in offering our unique Lifetime Consumer Satisfaction Guarantee: If you purchase an item featured in this Gift Guide, and at any point during your lifetime you become for any reason less than 100 percent satisfied with it, then *nyah, nyah, nyah.*

And we stand behind those words.

HIDEOUS REPUBLICAN PANTS

These were sent in by an alert reader seeking to get them out of the reach of her husband, who actually *wore* them, but you can obtain similar pants at fine thrift shops everywhere. Don't pay more than $2.

*a*s a member of the working classes, you've probably asked yourself many times what wealthy Republicans have that you don't have, aside from money. The answer is: color blindness. Yes. If you go to a country club frequented by wealthy Republicans and look at the clothes they wear when they're having Fun, you could suffer severe retina damage, so we advise against it. But you should definitely get a pair of pants like these for that Special Man on your gift list. Merely by putting these pants on, he will qualify for several major tax loopholes.

FAKE ARM

Around $11; found
in responsible joke
and novelty stores
everywhere.

So often we say to ourselves as shoppers, "I would like to give so-and-so something *practical*." Well, look no further, because this incredibly realistic Fake Arm is a gift that can be used in any number of everyday situations to "break the ice." For example, if you were going to a formal cocktail party, you could wear it sticking out from the fly of a pair of Hideous Republican Pants.

A LOCAL ELECTED OFFICIAL

*W*e are certain that often while doing
your holiday shopping you remark to yourself:
"I'd love to give somebody an elected official

18

this year, but they're just so darned *expensive.*"

Unfortunately, this is true at the Federal level. Purchasing a senator, or even a member of the House of Representatives, is beyond the price range of most people who do not have the good fortune to head failing savings-and-loan institutions. But don't overlook local politicians! There are some real bargains available on slightly used mayors, commissioners, and councilpersons, who will be happy to declare an Official Day or rename a street in honor of that Special Someone on your gift list. Or how about giving somebody a nice zoning variance? You'd be surprised how inexpensive it can be! Don't be shy! Make an offer! That's why we *have* public officials.

MEDICALLY ACCURATE MODEL of ONE POUND of FAT

$19.95; #H26030; Anatomical Chart Co., 8221 N. Kimball, Skokie, Ill. 60076-2956; phone 800-621-7500

This classic item was designed as an aid for professionals who, for some medical reason, need to show people what a pound of fat looks like. But we think it makes an ideal gift for the thoughtful hostess on your gift list. After she has served a gracious formal dinner to her guests, she could bring out an elegant dessert tray of fine pastries, arranged in an attractive display around the base of the pound of fat.

"Help yourselves to dessert," she could say, "bearing in mind that your body will almost instantly convert it into globs of this ugly pus-like substance." Yum!

BUG GUN

$3.25; Archie
McPhee, Box 30852,
Seattle, Wash. 98103;
phone 206-782-2344

*T*his is the first of a number of Gift Guide items we purchased from the Archie McPhee catalogue. In other catalogues, you see things you *want*, such as fine-quality matching leather luggage; but in the Archie McPhee catalogue, you see things you *need*, such as this Bug Gun. We are certain that several people on your gift list yearn to shoot insects across the room. Here is a gun designed *exactly for that purpose.* It comes with a set of rubber insects, but of course this is unnecessary where I live in South Florida, since you can usually catch a real insect merely by going outside and opening your mouth. We test-fired this gun in the *Miami Herald* newsroom, using an actual deceased South Florida Palmetto bug weighing four pounds, and the results were everything we had hoped for. Although we were somewhat surprised by the lawsuit.

MALL MADNESS

Around $35; Milton
Bradley Co.

*W*hat we love about the toy industry is the way it tries so hard to be educational. No doubt there have been many times when you've been sound asleep on a Saturday morning and you were suddenly awakened by your four-year-old, whose blood content is approaching 65 percent sugar as a result of eating Lucky Charms direct from the box, leaping up and down on your head and demanding that you immediately purchase all seventeen of the toys that were just advertised in a single commercial break on "The Smurfs," and you've said to yourself: "Thank goodness the toy industry is working hard to turn the nation's young people into Informed Consumers!"

Well, Mall Madness, a new board game, is a *big* help. It teaches what is probably the most important lesson that every young person should learn about life, namely: *The point of life is to buy a LOT of stuff.*

Mall Madness comes in a large box featuring pictures of happy little girls wearing about $17,000 worth of designer clothing apiece. The game board, which can be easily assembled in two days by anybody with a master's degree in engineering, is a three-dimensional miniature replica of a shopping mall. In the middle of the mall is an electronic device; when you push a button you hear The Voice of the Mall, which sounds like Pee-Wee Herman on steroids. The Voice of the Mall tells you how far you can move, and you race around the mall trying to buy things faster than your opponents do. It doesn't matter *what* you buy; the important thing is to *buy*.

Of course sometimes you run low on money, in which case you have to go to the bank, where, *merely for showing up*, you get free cash. "Take $100!" says The Voice of the Mall, generously. It's exactly like real life!

SPECIAL NOTE TO KIDS: If your parents don't buy you Mall Madness, it's because they don't love you.

ALLIGATOR SHOES

$12.95 per pair; they come in one size, which does not actually fit anybody; Archie McPhee, Box 30852, Seattle, Wash. 98103; phone 206-782-2344

These are definitely for the fashion-conscious person on your list who knows what kind of impression a person makes when he or she is wearing a pair of semirealistic rubber alligators on his or her feet. A BIG impression, that's what kind. You put these on, and instantly many members of the opposite sex are seized with the desire to have sexual relations with you. "Not now!" you find yourself constantly telling them. "I have to go shoot my Bug Gun!"

NINE-AND-A-HALF-INCH GLOW-IN-THE-DARK SQUID

$4.25; Archie McPhee, Box 30852, Seattle, Wash. 98103; phone 206-782-2344

*M*ore times than we can count we have found ourselves groping around in the dark, unable to locate our squid. But now, thanks to Modern Science, we have exactly the squid we need, one that is not only visible in total darkness, but also feels like a giant gob of mucus. The lucky person you give this to is bound to have a reaction.

CAN of PORK BRAINS

Manufactured by Armour, distributed by Dial Corp. Food Division, Phoenix, Ariz. 85077. Available wherever scary foods are sold. Sent in by alert reader Frank Gentry, who paid 53 cents for it.

This is certainly one of the most thoughtful gifts that we are including in the Gift Guide—a gift that simply says: "Here, take this can of pork brains." As you are no doubt aware, virtually every leading natural-disaster expert recommends that you keep a can of pork brains on hand, because there is no chance that you'll eat them except during a serious emergency, and probably not even then. This is a gift that will be handed down from generation to generation, like fruitcake.

MISTER DIP LIP

$85; #A79156;

Anatomical Chart Co.,

8221 N. Kimball,

Skokie, Ill.

60076-2956;

phone 800-621-7500

*a*s you may have guessed, this is brought to you by the same fun-loving folks who cooked up the Medically Accurate Model of One Pound of Fat. Mister Dip Lip is comparatively expensive, but there's an old saying that goes, "If you want a diseased artificial human mouth that is of high quality, you're going to have to pay for it."

Mister Dip Lip, which is made from a material that feels very much like the Glow-in-the-Dark

Squid, is a realistic replica of a human mouth that opens up, via levers in the back, to reveal, in vivid detail, the various alarming developments that can occur if you use tobacco products. It is intended for medical education, but we can think of many other practical uses. For example, you could keep valuables in Mister Dip Lip's mouth, because, trust us, nobody would ever reach in there. Or, if you knew somebody who was just about to wake up with a terrible hangover, you could creep into his bedroom, hold Mister Dip Lip's mouth one inch from his eyes, and then, while moving Mister Dip Lip's mouth levers, shout: "HI, BOB! WELCOME TO HELL!" This gift is too good to give away. Keep it yourself.

INDESTRUCTIBLE HOLIDAY FRUITCAKE FROM HELL

One of the most festive times of the Holiday Season is when Mr. or Ms. Mailperson comes grunting up the walk, and then *whump* drops a bulky parcel on your doorstep, creating a crater the size of a custom home spa.

"Ha, ha!" comes the jolly cry from every member of your family. "A fruitcake!"

Yes, it's a fruitcake, that very special, very dense holiday gift that some thoughtful person with the culinary sensibilities of a mulching machine always sends you, every year, year after year, despite the fact that nobody ever actually *eats* fruitcake. (Calvin Trillin, the great writer and food theoretician, once pointed this out in a column, and a bunch of people wrote him letters claiming that they did too eat fruitcake, and Trillin wrote another column saying, okay, maybe some misguided people have eaten fruitcakes, but nobody has ever *digested* one.)

So what can you do with your holiday gift fruitcake? Right! *You can give it to somebody else.* This is what many smart persons do. For maximum holiday revenge, you should wait a year and give it back to the person who gave it to you. "Take THIS," is the holiday message you are sending. Some fruitcakes have been passed back and forth for decades.

The problem, aside from widespread premature hernia-related mailperson deaths, is that even the toughest conventional fruitcake eventually shows signs of wear and tear. That's why, for our Gift Guide, we have decided to share with you our very special recipe for:

INDESTRUCTIBLE HOLIDAY FRUITCAKE FROM HELL:

Made with wholesome, 100 percent natural construction material, this baby is built to withstand any amount of holiday activity up to and including nuclear war.

Ingredients: Cement, fruit, water to taste

Directions: In a well-lit room wearing comfortable shoes, mix your cement and your water as directed on the bag and pour into a fruitcake-shaped container. Now mix in the fruit and allow to harden. Now simply send it via sturdy truck to that "special someone" on your holiday gift list. Do NOT attempt to lift it yourself.

RUBBER HOLIDAY SLUGS

For years we have kept a supply of these realistic rubber slugs on hand—we like to tie festive ribbons around their necks—for "last-minute" gift-giving. Let's say, for example, that you suddenly realize you forgot to purchase gifts for the large men who collect your garbage. You just grab a couple of these babies, rush out to the garbage truck, and generously shout: "Here, men! A slug for each of you!" (Do NOT stand in front of the truck when you shout this.)

36

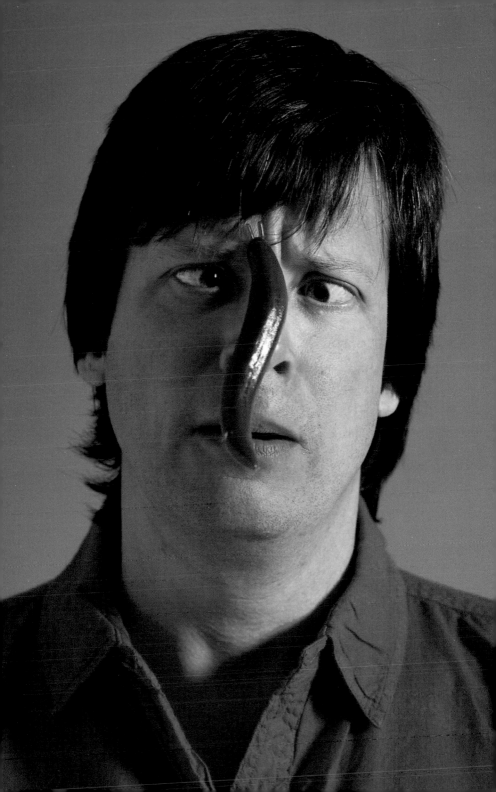

ROADKILL BINGO

$4.25, includes shipping; T-shirt is $12.00, includes shipping; game and T-shirt, $14.00; Creative Creations Co., P.O. Box 1343, Loveland, Colo. 80539-1343; phone 303-667-8636

This fun family game ("Providing Smiles for the Highway Miles") is the invention of the Matson Family, whom we would very much like to meet someday from a safe distance. According to the letter the Matsons sent us, "The game was invented after we kept a log of all the animals we saw along Interstate 80 in Nebraska and Iowa one summer." The game works pretty much like regular bingo, except that you look for deceased animals on the road, then put a marker over the picture of that animal on your card. As the instructions put it: "Remains to be seen if you are to get a bingo." (Ha, ha! Get it?)

The letter states that although "a few people are offended by the game," Roadkill Bingo "increases awareness of the roadside animals."

"You don't have to go to the Museum of Natural History to see wildlife," the letter adds.

Creative Creations Co. asserts that Roadkill Bingo "is great for stocking stuffers, graduation, going-away parties, and family reunions." We only hope that they come out with a South Florida version, where you also get credit for spotting deceased pedestrians or cars with bullet holes in the doors or confused Canadian motorists driving through hotel lobbies.

BALL of OWL VOMIT

Free; available wherever owls are vomiting.

This is the ideal gift for the nature-lover on your list. This particular item was suggested to us by Liz Nichols, a teacher who informs us that it is called an "owl pellet," and that owl scientists routinely collect and examine these things so that they will have an idea what owls are eating. We think this would be a wonderful conversation starter when boring guests come around. "Here!" you could say, thrusting it into their faces. "THIS should give you a good idea of what owls eat!"

HOLIDAY PET ANTLERS

$6.99; #380386; Pedigrees, 1989 Transit Way, Box 905, Brockport, N.Y. 14420-0905; phone 800-548-7486. Suggested by Ernest R. Irby Jr. of Richmond, Va., and Joyce Wolkomir of Montpelier, Vt.

One member of the family that you definitely don't want to forget during the gift-giving season is your pet. When you come home from work after a hard day, your loyal dog is always there to make you feel welcome by leaping up on you with insane joy and knocking you down and drooling all over your business clothes. Or, if you have a cat, it has probably spent the entire day feeling lonely and expressing its feelings by clawing your brand-new $979 reclining chair into tiny shreds.

How can you reward your pets for their year-round generosity? The best way we know of is to install these Holiday Pet Antlers on their heads. The antlers have a sturdy elastic strap and a little jingle bell that goes *JINGLE JIN-GLE JINGLE* every time your pet moves its head. Your pet will definitely look upon you with a joyful holiday expression that says, simply: "As soon as I figure out how to feed myself, I'm going to rip your lungs out."

OFFICER CULP

$24.75; NU-ERA, 727 N. 11th St., St.Louis, Mo. 63101; phone 800-325-7073. Suggested by Gretchen Schmidt of Coral Gables, Fla.

*W*e hate to dampen your mood, but crime is on the rise. Open any newspaper and you'll see stories about beatings, shootings, stabbings, muggings, kidnappings, fraud, conspiracy, racketeering, tax evasion, degeneracy, and perversion. And that's just in the *banking industry*.

The situation on our streets is even worse. Recently, a spokesperson for the Federal Bureau of Investigation, which uses a computer to compile monthly crime statistics on a state-by-state basis, announced that, during November 1993, *the computer was stolen.*

Clearly we cannot depend on the law-enforcement authorities to protect us. That is why security is a major concern of many of the people on your gift list, especially if they live in a high-crime district such as the Western Hemisphere. And the perfect gift for these people is: Officer Culp. Officer Culp is a life-size photograph of an actual model dressed up to look like an armed security officer. He is mounted on a backdrop of sturdy cardboard, with a big crease at waist level so that you can fold him over for easy transportation.

When unfolded, Officer Culp is astoundingly lifelike. We conducted a scientific experiment wherein we stood him up next to a real human City of Miami Beach Police Officer Harold Zeifman, and we found that it was virtually impossible to detect any differences between them, other than the fact that one of them (Officer Culp) was clearly made out of cardboard. As a further test, we had Officer Culp help Officer Zeifman direct traffic, using the technique of standing behind Officer Culp and waving our arms at cars in an authoritative manner. Most motorists made return hand gestures just as though Officer Culp were a real policeman.

We can think of many ways in which Officer Culp could be used to enhance personal security. When you park your car, you could stick him under your windshield wiper to scare off potential car thieves, especially if they are made out of cardboard. Or, if you're walking through a bad neighborhood, you could carry Officer Culp with you, chatting with him in a loud voice ("Officer Culp, have you lost weight? You're looking thin!"). This will protect you from muggers with tiny brains and incredibly bad eyesight.

We can personally vouch for the fact that Officer Culp gets the job done: We've had him "standing guard" at Gift Guide Headquarters for over a month, and during that time we have not had a *single bludgeoning death* that could not be attributed to natural causes.

WORMS EAT MY GARBAGE

$10.45, includes shipping; no credit cards; Flower Press, 10332 Shaver Rd., Kalamazoo, Mich. 49002; phone 616-327-0108. Suggested by Mary Barile of Arkville, N.Y.

*I*f you're looking for a gift for a literary person, the only logical choice is *Worms Eat My Garbage*, by Mary Appelhof. We don't want to give away the plot, but basically this book says you should keep a big box of worms around your house and feed your garbage to them. We are *not* making this up.

The purpose of your worm box is to help the

48

environment. Let's say you serve zucchini for supper, and naturally you have a lot of it left over, because the truth is that everybody secretly hates zucchini. So you dump it into your worm box, and the worms gobble it up, and before long you have a box full of compost (or, in scientific terms, "worm doody"), which you then use to organi-

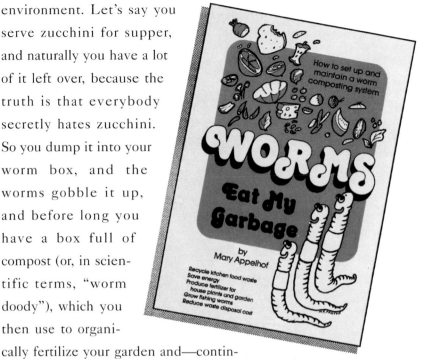

cally fertilize your garden and—continuing the Great Cycle of Life—grow *new* zucchini the size of Senator Howell Heflin.

Not only will you be saving the Earth, but you'll also be having a load of fun reading this entertaining book, which includes an entire chapter on the sex life of worms. Yes! Worms have sex lives! In fact, according to this book, all worms have *both male and female sexual organs*. It makes you wonder how they ever get anything done.

We would not be at all surprised to see *Worms Eat My Garbage* made into a major motion picture, starring The New Kids on the Block.

LAST SUPPER WALL CLOCK

$29.99; J9264;
Fingerhut Corporation,
11 McLeland Rd., St.
Cloud, Minn. 56395;
phone 800-233-3588.
Suggested by Laura
Watson of Spring
Creek, Tenn.

We are not saying that Mr. Leonardo da Vinci was not a heck of a painter, in his day. But like many top art critics, whenever we looked at Mr. da Vinci's painting of *The Last Supper*, we said to ourselves: "Darn it, something is *missing*."

But we could never put our finger on exactly what the problem was until we saw this beautiful Last Supper Wall Clock.

"That's it!" we said, smacking our foreheads so hard that we fell down. "It needed a *CLOCK!*"

Yes. Now you can combine the enjoyment of looking at *The Last Supper* with the practical value of knowing exactly what time it is, thanks to the inclusion of a battery-powered quartz clock in this beautiful reproduction, hovering in space just over the heads of some of the disciples. Leading historians agree that this is exactly what the actual Last Supper would have looked like if a giant battery-powered quartz clock had been present.

The painting comes with a decorative frame of the highest quality gold-colored plastic, which is so beautiful that even the most hardened interior decorator cannot look at it without weeping.

MODEL of DEFECTIVE NUCLEAR POWER PLANT

$13.98; #002000680; JMC International, 1025 Industrial Dr., Bensenville, Ill. 60106; phone 708-595-0210. Suggested by Donna Weistrop of Henderson, Nev.

*T*his gift item might help explain why the United States, in terms of technological "know-how," is falling behind Japan, Europe, and the Amazonian Mud People. What we have here is an educational model of a nuclear power plant, which comes in a kit that young people are supposed to assemble. So far, so good. The problem is that, according to the Edmund Scientific catalogue, this kit is "based on Three Mile Island." That's right: Of all the nuclear power plants they

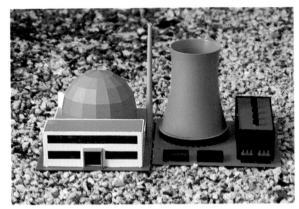

could have selected to educate our children, they picked the one that threatened to turn southeastern Pennsylvania into a giant uranium fondue. We are wondering if this will be part of a whole new line of Defective Educational Toys, including a model of the Hubble Space Telescope or a Vice President Quayle Action Figure.

Nevertheless, we believe the Three Mile Island kit would be an excellent gift for the young person on your list who has an active imagination to the point of needing to attend a special school. Think of the fun this youngster will have assembling the reactor, then, with the aid of a blowtorch *(sold separately)*, creating a "meltdown" that causes thousands of little plastic local residents *(sold separately)* to flee or risk being mutated into Blob People, who would scream and scream in an educational fashion until it was time for the lucky youngster to receive his or her Special Medicine *(sold separately)*.

CREATIVE USES for DEAD SPORTSMEN'S ASHES

Various prices, depending on what you want; Canuck's Sportsman's Memorials Inc., P.O. Box 4052, Des Moines, Iowa 50333; phone 515-244-8631. Suggested by Dawn Price and Sheila Mauck of Des Moines, Iowa, who sent in a *Des Moines Register* article about this, written by Jim Pollock.

*T*his is the ultimate gift concept for the sportsman on your list who is no longer able to enjoy hunting or fishing because he has, unfortunately, kicked the bucket. If you give the sportsman's cremated remains to Canuck's Sportsman's Memorials, they will, for a price, load the ashes in a shotgun shell, take the shell on a hunting trip, and shoot it at a duck or other game animal of your choice. We swear we are *not* making this up.

We called the president of Canuck's

Sportsman's Memorials, Jay W. Knudsen Sr. and he told us that, in addition to converting sportsmen into ammunition, his company also offers a wide variety of other "unique and different methods of ash dispersion."

For example, he said, the ashes of one deceased former hunter will be placed in some duck decoys, which will then be used by the man's former hunting companions.

"The decoys will bob among the ones that he used to use," says Knudsen. "He will be right in the decoy display."

Knudsen said that one fisherman, still alive, wants his ashes placed inside fishing lures, which his family members "will then use for the rest of their lives."

We're not sure that our idea of a dignified post-life is to have our Earthly remains constantly being swallowed and spit out by bass. Nevertheless, we think this is a truly wondrous, uniquely *American* gift concept, and we strongly recommend it.

By the way, the Canuck's Sportsman's Memorials motto is: "We can't get you to heaven, but we can land you in the Happy Hunting Ground."

RUDE NOISE SLIPPERS

$$W$$

e can only speculate about how this amazing gift idea became a reality. Probably some top research scientists were sitting around in their laboratory, trying to think up scientific breakthroughs, and one of them, after accidentally inhaling some test-tube fumes, sat up and said: "Wait a minute! What if we combined a PAIR OF SLIPPERS with a WHOOPEE CUSHION?"

It was a Giant Step Forward for mankind, every bit as significant as the moment, hundreds of thousands of years ago, when some primitive genius

$12.98; #T3850; Funny Side Up, 425 Stump Rd., North Wales, Pa. 19454; phone 215-361-5142. Suggested by Dick Hakes of Storm Lake, Iowa.

carved the first crude wheel out of stone, and attached a whoopee cushion to it. This is the kind of historic item we're talking about, and it would make the perfect gift for that distinguished gentleman or lady on your list who likes to come home after a hard day, put on a comfortable pair of slippers, and walk around the house making loud flatulence noises with his or her feet.

We've tested these babies in the office, and they work beautifully. The whoopee cushion is in the heel of the right slipper, so when you walk around, you go *(step)* BLATT *(step)* BLATT *(step)* BLATT. We can't tell you how relaxing this is. We wouldn't be surprised if members of the U.S. Supreme Court use these slippers to unwind in their chambers. We just hope they remember to remove them before entering the courtroom ("All rise!" [*step*] BLATT [*step*] BLATT . . .).

One size sort of fits all.

GIANT FIBERGLASS GOOSE

$385; Fiberglass Products, P.O. Box 340, Ft. Pierre, S.D. 57532; phone 605-223-2120; allow 2 to 3 weeks for delivery before hunting season. Suggested by Bob Garber of Washington, D.C.

*F*or a while, in preparing this Gift Guide, we were beginning to despair of ever finding the "ultimate" gift concept. But the moment we saw this item, we became so excited that we put our head down on our desk and drooled all over our telephone-message slips with joy. For we knew that, at last, we had found the *pièce de résistance* (French, meaning, "big false bird").

This spectacular item is an imitation goose

that looks exactly like a real goose in every respect except that it's made out of fiberglass and is the size of a forklift. It has a hinge on its side that permits the top of the goose to swing open so that a hunter can get inside.

We gather that the hunter and his dog are supposed to crouch inside the giant goose, hiding, and some *real* geese, migrating down from Canada, are supposed to come flying along and look down and think: "Hey! There's a goose down there! It must be safe to land!"

The only problem we have with this scenario is that, if *we* were a real goose, and we looked down and saw a giant mutant goose appearing to weigh well over a thousand pounds, we wouldn't go anywhere *near* it. We'd immediately sound the Emergency Honk and migrate the hell on back to Canada.

So if the Giant Fiberglass Goose actually works, the only possible explanation is that geese are the second-stupidest species on Earth. The *stupidest* species, of course, is anybody who would get inside the Giant Fiberglass Goose with a dog.

However, we do feel that this item has many practical uses that make it the ideal gift for the person on your gift list who wants to conduct discreet surveillance without drawing attention to him- or herself. We had our crack Gift Research Team field-test the giant goose by taking it around the Miami area and using it in various real-life surveillance situations. The team reported that the goose was highly effective. It drew virtually no attention, other than motorists slamming on their brakes, thousands of passersby staring, and a constant stream of people walking up and saying: "What the heck is THAT?"

The Research Team also went to the beach, and they reported that the giant goose was an extremely effective device for starting conversations with hot-looking babes.

"They were just *walking up* to us," stated the team. "They *really liked* the goose."

This makes us think that the giant goose might be an ideal gift for the single man on your list. He could walk into a singles bar, casually set his goose down, order a drink, and wait for an attractive woman to strike up a conversation: "Say! That's a BIG goose you have there, fella!"

PRIVATE COW PARTS

$42.15; LS2798; Nasco, P.O. Box 901, Fort Atkinson, Wis. 53538-0901; phone 800-558-9595. Suggested by James J. Allen of Coral Springs, Fla.

𝒯his gift idea can be purchased via the Nasco mail-order catalogue, which features products that farmers need to engage in acts of agriculture. We have to admit that, when we first saw this particular item, our reaction was that it was too offensive *even for the Gift Guide*. To help you understand why we felt this way, here's the complete catalogue description:

Preserved Reproductive Tract of Cow: Ideal for instruction of the manipulative process in artificial insemination, and the study of the gross anatomy of the female reproductive system. Complete tract including ovaries, oviducts, uterus, vagina, bladder, and external organ. Preserved with a patented, odorless, nontoxic solution (not formaldehyde). Can be kept in a plastic bag and used repeatedly for long periods of time.

We have nothing but the deepest respect for the American cow farmer, but when we read things like this, we have to ask ourselves if maybe he hasn't been struck in the head by a few too many falling hay bales. We were frankly shocked that anybody might actually want to own a set of intimate organs that at one time were part of a real, mooing cow, let alone use them "repeatedly for long periods of time."

But we decided to order it anyway, because we are great bargain-hunters, and you rarely see a *complete* cow reproductive tract at a price this low. When it arrived, we realized what a wise decision we had made, because this is easily the most disgusting thing we have ever seen, and bear in mind that we regularly watch "Geraldo." We have had our cow reproductive tract—nicknamed "Bossy"—at Gift Guide Headquarters for more than two months, and we have not found a *single person* who can look directly at it.

We can think of a number of practical nonagriculture applications for an item like this. Let's say some relatives you hate show up unannounced at your house, expecting to stay with you for a couple of days. You say: "Sure!" Then you lead them into the guest room, and there, on the bed, is: Bossy.

"Marge!" you shout to your spouse. "There's another one of those things in the guest room!"

"Darn!" says Marge. "No sooner do we get rid of one, but another one shows up!"

"Don't worry," you say to the relatives. "We rarely get more than two or three per night, so maybe you won't . . . What, you're leaving already?"

DO NOT OPEN EVER

Bossy would also do a superb job of saving your seat in a movie theater. Or, if you were taking an airplane trip, you could pull Bossy out of your briefcase and guarantee that you'd have a whole row of seats to yourself. You could even change the plane's destination. ("Take us to the Bahamas, Captain, or I'll *show you that thing again.*") You could also avoid spending thousands of dollars on a fancy electronic home-security system simply by placing Bossy in a guard position near your front door, and installing a sign outside ("WARNING: THESE PREMISES PROTECTED BY REPRODUCTIVE TRACT OF COW").

We could go on and on talking about the many possible uses for this unique holiday idea, but we are going to be sick.

HIGH-TECH PRANK RAT

$30 from Fast Buck Freddie's, 500 Duval St., Key West, Fla. 33040; phone 305-294-2007. Suggested by Jean De St. Croix of Marathon Shores, Fla., who found it at Fast Buck Freddie's in the back room on the left between the rack of dirty birthday cards and the display of transparent telephones with fluorescent innards. Jean adds: "I personally have friends who would kill for a nice gift like this."

*O*ne of the blessings of living in the Space Age is that we are able to enhance our life-styles with highly advanced technology. Nowhere is this more evident than in the field of prank rats. Years ago, the typical prank rat was a passive lump of rubber. You tossed it into the lap of the victim, and the most you could hope for was a shriek, maybe some minor permanent heart damage.

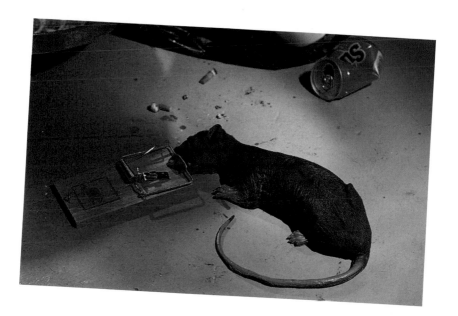

All that has changed with the introduction of Rat-in-the-Trap, an amazingly lifelike latex unit that contains not only a battery-powered motor, but also a sonic mechanism, which we believe was developed by the National Aeronautics and Space Administration for use in prank rats that are carried aboard the space shuttle.

When you make a noise, such as whistling or clapping your hands, the sonic mechanism activates the motor, and the rat starts squirming around in an *extremely* realistic manner with its snout in the trap. You can almost see little motorized plague-carrying fleas scurrying around on that rat's back as it writhes its way across the floor. In a properly planned prank, this rat could induce full cardiac arrest at a *minimum*. It's the most hideous, disgusting, revolting performance we have ever seen by any entity that did not have a law degree.

AUTO SECURITY SPIDER

$6.95; RSP100; Aahs!!,
3223 Wilshire Blvd.,
Santa Monica, Calif.
90403;
phone 310-829-1807

*C*onsider this: In the United States, an automobile is stolen every 14.7 seconds.

If that statistic scares you, think how we felt when we made it up. Because we were fully aware that the actual statistic could be even worse.

That's why chances are there's somebody on your gift list who would like nothing better than to receive a quality car-security device. But which one?

Probably the best-known car-security device is "The Club." This product is advertised extensively via a TV commercial wherein a person claiming to be a police officer tells you that he's standing on a spot from which a car has just been stolen.

What bothers us about this commercial is this: If the police officer knows the car has just been stolen, *why isn't he doing anything about it?* Why is he just standing there, yammering away about The Club? Is that what the taxpayers are paying him to do? Shouldn't he be chasing the car thief? Or could it be that— we don't want to start rumors, but we have to consider every possibility—the thief has stolen *the police officer's car?*

In that case, we have to ask ourselves if The Club is really all it's cracked up to be. We have to ask ourselves if there is perhaps ANOTHER car-security product on the market that would offer superior automotive protection, PLUS certain other useful qualities such as being able to float in a swimming pool.

Fortunately, there IS such a product: The Spider. This is a high-quality piece of limp plastic that can be easily wadded into a standard glove compartment. When you park your car, you simply remove The Spider, spend a pleasant and relaxing ten or fifteen minutes blowing it up, and *voilà* (French, meaning, "eek"), you have a large inflated arachnid on your hands.

To arm your security device, you simply fashion The Spider's legs around your steering wheel. You can now walk away in a carefree manner, knowing that even the most hardened professional thief is going to think twice before messing with your vehicle. He'll take one look at The Spider and wisely elect to move on to a more vulnerable car, such as one protected by The Hamster.

We are not just blowing smoke when we make these claims. We tested The Spider in a "real-world" environment involving an actual car. We observed the car for a full minute, and absolutely nothing happened—despite printed statistics indicating that, during that time, the average car should have been stolen *four times*.

But there's more: The Spider can also be used as a personal security device. Yes. If you find yourself in a neighborhood frequented by violent criminals, simply inflate The Spider, fasten it around your neck, and stroll confidently on your way as the criminals give you a wide berth, for fear of coming in contact with your saliva.

COMPARISON CHART: THE SPIDER vs. THE CLUB

	THE CLUB	THE SPIDER
PRICE	Over $50	$6.95
INFLATABILITY	No	Yes
NUMBER OF LEGS	None	Eight
MEAN-LOOKING EYEBALLS?	No	Yes
FEMALE EATS MALE AFTER MATING?	No	Yes

BULL SCROTUM

$35; Goode Company Barbeque, 8911 Katy Freeway, Houston, Tex. 77024; phone 713-464-1901

*L*adies, here's a unique item that's bound to cause the men on your gift-giving list to wince with joy.

We found this item in the great state of Texas (motto: "Where Good Taste Originated Someplace

Else"). We were in Houston, at a cafeteria-style restaurant called Goode Company Barbeque, and when we brought our tray to the cashier, we saw, hanging overhead, a large selection of these odd-looking *things*. At first we thought they might be some kind of rare hairy prairie coconuts. But when we read the label and found out what they were, we were so overcome by excitement that we nearly dropped our pork platter. Because this item, according to the label, is "an actual scrotum of the King of the Range."

That's right: This is an extremely personal private part that somebody was able to obtain—we don't even want to *think* about how—from an actual bull. Judging from the size of this item, the bull was an *extremely* masculine animal. We've been in a lot of major-league locker rooms in our day, and we have never seen anything *approaching* the capacity of this particular item, as measured in cubic feet. So we think it would be the perfect gift for a woman to give to that "special man" to express the romantic message: "Darling, this reminds me of you, only much larger."

(We understand that Sylvester Stallone has fourteen of these.)

The bull scrotum also has many practical uses around the home. You can put things into it. You can even wear it on your head, assuming you have a certain amount of what the French call *joie de vivre* (literally, "soybean curd for brain").

Each bull scrotum comes with a convenient leather carrying strap so you don't have to touch it. Don't be fooled by cheap imitations. This is the *only* bull scrotum endorsed by the League of Women Voters *and* the Rev. Pat Robertson.

WORM BLOWER

Around $1.40—shipping is $3.50; manufactured by Lindy-Little Joe Inc., Box C, 1110 Wright St., Brainerd, Minn. 56401; phone 218-829-1714. Suggested by John Cahill of Alexandria, Va. Also available locally.

a fisherperson's worm says a lot about him. When he's out fishing with his buddies, he does not want to reach into his bait bucket, grope around, and pull out a pale, limp, flaccid worm; he wants a worm he can be proud of, a vibrant, glistening, throbbing worm, a worm that will cause the buddies to spit enviously and say: "Whoa! Check out NORM'S worm."

And the fisherperson on your gift list will be

sure of having the night crawler of his dreams every time, if you give him this Worm Blower from the Lindy line of fine fishing accessories. As the package states:

"Blowing up a crawler not only keeps it off the bottom, but can make a skimpy, shriveled up crawler look like a super worm."

Basically, the worm blower is a plastic squeeze bottle with a syringe-type needle on it. The sportsperson simply sticks the needle into the worm, squeezes the bottle, and, *voilà*, the worm explodes.

No, ideally that does not happen, although apparently it is a danger, because the directions state:

SQUEEZE WORM BLOWER BEING CAREFUL NOT TO RUPTURE CRAWLER.

But we still think the worm blower is a very thoughtful gift idea for any man who is concerned about the size and perkiness of his worm.

(We understand that Sylvester Stallone has twenty-two of these.)

RUBBER CHICKEN

$8.95; Archie McPhee, Box 30852, Seattle, Wash. 98103; phone 206-782-2344

*L*ike most shoppers, you have said to yourself many times, "Sure, I would like to give a rubber chicken, but how can I be sure of the quality?" Well, we are here to vouch personally for this model of chicken. Once, for a story on scuba diving, we spent thirty minutes on the bottom of a swimming pool with this chicken impaled on the end of our spear gun, and it did not give us a speck of trouble. As the Archie McPhee catalogue states: "Not the cheap Far East knockoff, but a rubber chicken in the classic tradition of Europe."

CHRISTOPHER COLUMBUS TRICK CANDY

Card of 6 is $1.95, minimum order $10; manufactured by Accoutrements; available to consumers from Archie McPhee, Box 30852, Seattle, Wash. 98103; phone 206-782-2344. Suggested by Katy Spear of San Jose, Calif.

*W*e will come right out and say it: This is one of our absolute all-time favorite Gift Guide items, and that statement includes the Giant Fiberglass Goose. This item is so wonderful that we're STILL not convinced that it originated on the planet Earth.

The best way for you to appreciate this item is if we just quote, verbatim, the information on the package, which we swear we are not making up:

QUALITY . . . SINCE 1492,

CHRISTOPHER COLUMBUSBRAND TRICK CANDY

Looks like candy . . . but open one up and EEEE! Vermin! Hidden inside each wrapper is a quality rubber mouse, bug, spider, or snake. This same joke was used during the voyage to the New World to keep the crew amused.

This makes a lot of sense to us. We can just imagine the tense situation on that fateful voyage 500 years ago:

For weeks the ships have been sailing into the unknown, with the safety of home far, far behind. As supplies dwindle and no sign of land appears on the vast, empty ocean, the crew becomes restive, nagged by the growing, cold, gut-clenching fear that they're being led to their deaths. Finally a mob of angry sailors confronts Columbus, threatening to mutiny if he doesn't turn back. With nerves stretched to the breaking point, and the threat of violence hanging heavy in the air, Columbus offers the men some candy. Hesitantly, suspiciously, they open the bright foil wrappers and EEEE!

Ha, ha! Instantly the tension is broken as the men gaily pelt each other with quality rubber vermin.

CAP SHAPER

$3.95; Carol Wright Gifts,
340 Applecreek Rd.,
Lincoln, Neb. 68544;
phone 402-474-5174.
Suggested by Kathryn
Godlewski of Racine, Wis.

*B*aseball-style caps present a real cleaning challenge to the conscientious homemaker.

One major challenge, of course, is getting the cap off of the head of the person who wears it. We do not wish to single out any specific gender here, but a lot of men NEVER take their caps off—not in restaurants, not at funerals, not in bed, not while undergoing brain surgery.

And even if you DO get the owner to remove the cap, you find that it's encrusted with a thick layer of grime that has been formed into a kind of mortar by dried sweat. This poses a real cleaning problem, and until recently the only proven way to solve it was to make a paste mixture of baking soda and kerosene, rub it thoroughly into the cap, then set fire to it.

The problem with this approach is that then the man has to go get a whole new cap, and some models—especially the ones with advanced features such as the adjustable brim—can run as high as $2.79. But fortunately it is no longer necessary to lay out that kind of money, thanks to the amazing new Cap Shaper.

We can't understand how come, in a supposedly advanced country, it took so long for somebody to think this up. What it is, basically, is a plastic thing that you put a cap in so that you can wash the cap *in the dishwasher*. Then you just run your dishwasher normally, and bang, all that icky grime has been washed off the cap and spewed all over your silverware. So maybe you'd better wash the cap all by itself.

We think this is a terrific product concept, and we are hoping to see new items added to the Shaper line, including the Sock Shaper, the Shoe Shaper, and the Jockstrap Shaper. Eventually we may see the day when you can wash ALL your clothes in the dishwasher, and somebody will develop products that enable you to wash your dishes in the washing machine.

PINEAPPLE UTILITY LIGHT

*I*t's often been said that you can never find a utility light when you need one, and the same is certainly true of pineapples. That's why we know some lucky person on your gift list will be thrilled to receive this item. To make it, simply take a battery-powered utility light (we got

ours for $2.97 at Home
Depot) and screw it onto a
nice fresh pineapple (about
$1.50) to create a gift that
is sure to find a perma-
nent home on the recipi-
ent's bedside table. Let the
blackout come! When the
lights go out, all the recipient
has to do is reach out and suffer moderately severe skin lac-
erations! This is a gift that keeps
on giving.

HIGH-TECH LOUDSPEAKER HAT

$14.95; American Science and Surplus, 3605 Howard St., Skokie, Ill. 60202; phone 708-982-0870.

You need this item. Everybody who sees this item in action at the Gift Guide Headquarters immediately says: "Hey, I NEED one of those."

And no wonder. This is a plastic hat with a battery-powered loudspeaker mounted on the top and a microphone dangling down. If you press a button on the side of the microphone and speak into it, your amplified voice comes out of the loudspeaker on top of your head with *incredibly low fidelity*. That alone would make this item worth owning, but there's another switch on the microphone, and you can use it to make *three kinds of siren noises*.

Trust us, when you put this hat on, everybody pays attention to you. You have a distinct advantage over ordinary humans, most of whom don't even have loudspeakers, let alone sirens. We think the president of the United States should wear one of these hats to give him an "edge" when he meets with foreign heads of state for high-level negotiations.

U.S. PRESIDENT (through his loudspeaker): And another thing. We want you to leave the Kurds ALONE.

SADDAM HUSSEIN: Now wait just a minute. You're talking about the internal affairs of a . . .

U.S. PRESIDENT (turning on his siren): *WOOOP WOOOP WOOOP WOOOP* . . .

SADDAM HUSSEIN: OK! OK!

This hat is also great for communicating at loud cocktail parties. And successful businesspersons tell us that wearing this hat around the office greatly enhances their stature. (We understand that H. Ross Perot owns 4,000 of these.)

BUDWEISER SLIPPERS

$29.98; Taylor Gifts, 355 E. Conestoga Rd., P.O. Box 206, Wayne, Pa. 19087-0206; phone 215-293-3613. Early versions originally suggested by Annette Eubank of Gardenville, Pa., and Tom Ward of Fall River, Mass.

*D*id you ever wonder what your leading tasteful fashion designers such as Mr. Oscar "D" La Renta do when they get home after a hard day of designing clothes that ordinary dirtball humans such as yourself cannot afford? The answer is, they kick off their shoes and put on a pair of slippers shaped like giant Budweiser cans. Yes! Budweiser Slippers are all the rage this year in both New York and Paris.

(We understand that Ms. Ivana Trump owns forty-six pairs.)

You may recall our Gift Guide also features slippers that make a flatulent sound when trod upon. Now we have Budweiser Slippers. This rapid advance in slipper technology—and by the way, Japan is *years* behind the United States in this area—makes us wonder what amazing development the slipper industry will spring on us next. Cappuccino-machine slippers? Drill-press slippers? Slippers containing a combination fax machine and ant farm? This is a great time to be alive.

DUCK BUTTS

$7.59 per pair; Knutson's Recreational Sales Inc., 164 Wamplers Lake Rd., Box 457, Brooklyn, Mich. 49230; phone 800-248-9318. Suggested by Phil Smith of Richmond, Va.

*I*f you have a sportsperson on your gift list, the chances are excellent that he would love to have a Duck Butt.

And no wonder. As you are no doubt aware, a major problem with traditional duck decoys is that they are all in the upright position; whereas *real* ducks periodically stick their heads underwater to look for snails or car keys or whatever it is that ducks are looking for underwater.

This means that if you have a set of ordinary decoys, all in the upright position, they don't look natural. Ducks flying overhead are eventually going to become suspicious.

"Hey," they are going to say. "How come those so-called 'ducks'

down there are all in the upright position?"

Granted, this probably will not happen until several billion years from now, when ducks have evolved to the point where they can talk. But it never hurts to be prepared, which is why we're certain that the sportsperson on your list will be thrilled to receive this gift, which is an exact replica of a duck butt, weighted so the tail sticks up. This will definitely lend an aura of realism to any decoy flotilla, thus attracting the attention of real ducks flying overhead. ("Hey! How come some of those so-called 'ducks' down there never come up for air?")

Bonus Tip for Home Entertainers: These duck butts can also add "a touch of class" to a punch bowl.

INSPIRATIONAL NIGHT LIGHT

$3.95; Carol Wright Gifts, 340 Applecreek Rd., Lincoln, Neb. 68544; phone 402-474-5174.

*J*f you're in the market for a tasteful night light shaped like a major religious figure— and who isn't?—this is the item for you.

We're not making any claims about this nightlight having special powers. We're not suggesting, for

example, that if you brush your teeth in front of this nightlight, YOUR GUM PROBLEMS WILL BE MIRACULOUSLY HEALED! Or that the rays from this nightlight can PERMANENTLY ELIMINATE UNWANTED BODILY HAIR! Nor would we suggest that this nightlight can IMPROVE YOUR LOVE LIFE! and cause you to WIN THE STATE LOTTERY! as well as LOSE UP TO 75 POUNDS IN TWO WEEKS WITHOUT DIETING!

It's just a nightlight, that's all, and you should feel free to disregard the fact that MR. RALPH WHELKMONGER OF AKRON, OHIO, DECIDED NOT TO BUY THIS NIGHT LIGHT, AND THE NEXT DAY HE WAS DISMEMBERED IN A FREAK FERRIS WHEEL ACCIDENT.

THOSE AMAZING LEECHES

$13.95; by Cheryl M. Halton, Macmillan Publishing Company, 100 Front St., Box 500, Riverside, N.J. 08075-7500; phone 800-257-5755. Suggested by Topher Gee of Medford, Mass.

One look at the cover of this Gift Guide Literary Selection tells you why it was included: It features two large leeches sitting on a human foot, cheerfully sucking blood out of a toe that has some kind of repulsive purplish inflammation.

"Yum," the leeches are clearly thinking.

Yes, if there is a friend or loved one on your gift list who has a hankering to know more—*much* more—about slime-covered bloodsucking

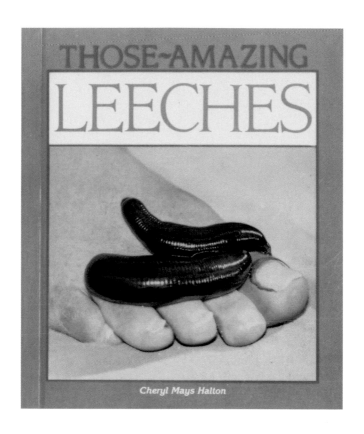

THOSE-AMAZING
LEECHES

Cheryl Mays Halton

parasites, we cannot think of a more appropriate gift than this book. It contains many Amazing Leech Facts—did you know, for example, that some leeches grow to be *more than a foot long?*—and it has chapters entitled "A Visit to a Leech Farm" and "Collecting and Keeping Leeches." This is an opportunity for the science-minded young person on your gift list to get into the fast-growing hobby of leech breeding. ("Mom, I can't find Rex." "Well, where did you see him last?" "Crawling into Jessica's nose." "*EEEE!*")

COW PARTS GAME

$16.50; #C8432;
Nasco,
P.O. Box 901,
Fort Atkinson, Wis.
53538-0901; phone
800-558-9595.

*W*hen you are talking about riotous party fun, you are talking about trying to name the parts of a dairy cow. That is the idea behind this exciting game. There can be up to six players, each of whom is represented by a different breed of cow, such as Holstein, Ayrshire, etc. As they (the players) move around the playing board, they must correctly identify the cow parts

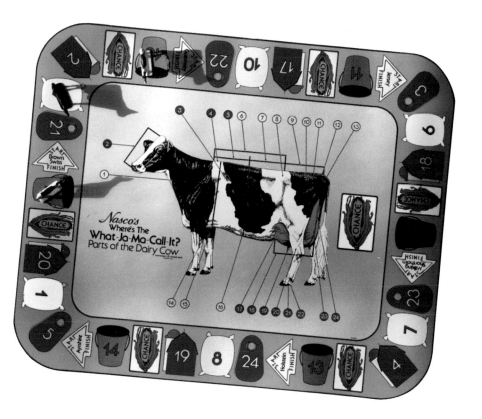

indicated on each of the spaces. These parts include the "dewlap," the "pastern," the "fore udder attachment," the "median suspensory ligament," the "hock," the "stifle," and, of course, the "teats."

We are certain that the host or hostess on your gift list would be thrilled to receive this item, which is sure to get any social occasion moving. ("It's 1:30 a.m.! Aren't these people *ever* going to go home?" "I know! Let's get out the Cow Parts Game!")

CHIN FIRMER

**$4.99; #N3168;
Walter Drake and
Sons, 53 Drake
Building, Colorado
Springs, Colo. 80940;
phone 719-596-3853.
Suggested by Jessica
Bernstein of
Alexandria, Va.**

*M*ost employers will tell you that the most important factor that they consider when making decisions about hiring and promotions is chin firmness. That is why this chin-firming device is the ideal gift for everyone on your gift list who is looking to "get ahead," particularly in those jobs where personal appearance is critical, such as TV anchorperson, U.S. senator, ballerina, and astronaut.

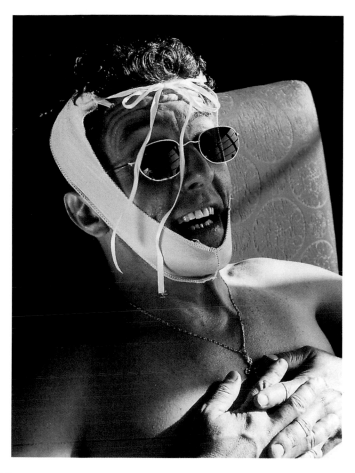

The beauty of this device is that it can be worn anywhere and will be virtually unnoticed except for the fact that it covers a large part of the face and head. Thus the person looking for chin improvement can keep this device on for great lengths of time. It is our understanding that Gen. Norman Schwarzkopf virtually never took his off when he was directing military operations in the Persian Gulf.

BEAUTY MASK

$3.89; #0689-4;
Miles Kimball, 41 W.
Eighth Ave., Oshkosh,
Wis. 54906; phone
414-231-4886.
Suggested by Roz
Marottoli of New
Haven, Conn.

*H*ere is a practical idea for the person on your gift list who takes pride in her or his appearance. This is a hood that covers the wearer's entire head, like a beekeeper's hood. The purpose, according to the catalogue, is "to protect your hairdo and keep your makeup from smearing" while you're getting dressed.

But why stop there? Why run the risk that

your hairdo and makeup might get mussed AFTER you are dressed? We here at the Gift Guide Headquarters believe that a person who truly wants to look his or her best will simply leave the Beauty Mask hood on at all times, even on dates, unzipping it only when it is necessary to insert food, or spit. For maximum protection, we feel that the Beauty Mask should be left on *even during sex*. ("Oh, Marcia, that feels so . . . HEY! Who IS this?" "This is Ed! Who is THIS?")

INTERNAL REVENUE SERVICE CHRISTMAS-TREE ORNAMENT

$11; The Treasury Historical Association, P.O. Box 28118, Washington, D.C. 20038-8118; phone 202-895-5250. Suggested by Miriam Howe of Crownsville, Md.

*T*his item is so wonderful that we feel obligated to remind you we are *not* making it up. This is a Christmas-tree ornament created to mark the eightieth anniversary of the establishment of the income tax. It's gold-plated metal, and it depicts a 1913 IRS form (which was one page). At the bottom it says: "Eighty Years of Income Tax" and "Many Happy Returns." (Ha, ha! Get it?)

This unique gift idea was created by the Treasury Historical Association, a nonprofit organization that will use the proceeds to purchase new cattle prods for needy IRS agents.

No, we are kidding. The proceeds will be used to help restore the Old Treasury Building in Washington, D.C. This is certainly a worthy cause, so you will want to purchase this ornament for a special taxpayer on your gift list. Remember, however, that if you do not order this ornament in time for holiday gift-giving, you MUST order Extension Ornament 2093-3J on or before the sixth fiscal week of the holiday season unless you are a joint taxpayer giving gifts singly. If we were you, we would contact our lawyer immediately.

TONGUE CLEANER

$4.95 (plus shipping and handling); The Mystic Trader, 1334 Pacific Ave., Forest Grove, Ore. 97116; phone 800-634-9057. Suggested by Dana Preston of Santa Rosa, Calif.

*M*ost of us rarely give any thought to cleaning our tongues. Yet each year more than 34 million Americans develop physical problems that could easily have been prevented with adequate tongue hygiene, according to statistics that recently came to us in a dream.

This is hardly surprising when you consider the kinds of things you routinely put into your mouth, such as peanut butter, Chinese food,

pizza, gumbo, and clams. Most of these things slide down into your stomach, where they are broken down by amino acids and turned into useful body parts, except of course for the clams, which are expelled from your body untouched and often go on to lead long and healthy lives in the sewer system. But a certain amount of food residue remains on your tongue. Over the years, layer upon layer of this residue—scientists call it "crud"—builds up, and eventually it becomes disgusting. Of course you are unaware of this. What with the demands of career and family, you rarely have time to examine your tongue. But believe us: your friends, family, and coworkers see your tongue all the time, and they are really grossed out.

"Did you SEE that??" they ask each other as soon as you leave the room. "It looks like [*your name*] is trying to swallow the creature from the motion picture *Aliens III*!"

That is why we strongly recommend that you purchase this tongue cleaner for yourself and every person whom you truly care about on your gift-giving list. The Mystic Trader catalogue states that tongue cleaners have been "used in Eastern countries for over 2,000 years." We are not making this quotation up. We are also not certain whether it means that people in these Eastern countries have been using the *same* tongue cleaners for 2,000 years, or whether the tongue cleaners are changed regularly. Either way, we consider this a powerful argument for this item, because if there is one thing that Eastern countries have always been associated with, it is clean tongues.

Top entertainment figures such as Clint Eastwood and Zsa

Zsa Gabor—people who have professional interest in looking their best—never finish a meal at a swank Hollywood restaurant without immediately, right at their tables, having their tongues cleaned by their personal assistants. You and the people on your gift list may not have personal assistants, but you can certainly look just as good. Even better, in the case of Zsa Zsa.

FLAME JET WEEDER

$14.95; Carol Wright Gifts, 340 Applecreek Rd., Lincoln, Neb. 68544-8503; phone 402-474-5174.

Suggested by Nathan M. Brooks of Arlington, Va.

This is the perfect gift idea for the person who has:

1. A garden or yard.

2. Insurance.

What this item is, basically, is a blowtorch with a long metal tube attached. This means that, instead of having to bend all the way over and

pull out those nasty weeds by hand, you simply fire up your Flame Jet Weeder and stride around your garden or yard, incinerating weeds, insects, worms, squirrels, small dogs, and any other life form in your path. If you have an adolescent son, we're betting he'll be MORE than willing to do a LOT of yard work if he can use the Flame Jet Weeder, thereby freeing you to relax and watch TV until it's time to call the fire department.

We think this could also be the ideal item for the single man on your gift list who would like to be able to pick up women in bars by lighting their cigarettes from as many as three bar stools away. ("Here, allow me . . . WHOOPS!" "EEEKK!! MY HAIR!!!!" "Sorry!")

HEAD LICE COLORING BOOK

*N*ever before have we encountered a gift idea for children that was so reasonably priced and yet involved parasites. This is a very attractive twelve-page coloring book about head lice, sold by the National Pediculosis Association ("pediculosis" is the medical term for "coloring

$.25 each, minimum order is 25; the National Pediculosis Association, P.O. Box 149, Newton, Mass. 02161; phone 800-446-4672

book"). Its pages depict the activities of a group of lice who arrive on a human head and settle in. ("We glue our eggs to your hair," they state.) It also explains how the child can get rid of these pesky creatures via a simple medical technique involving the Flame Jet Weeder.

No! Just kidding! The coloring book contains safe medical advice. We are certain that this item will provide the youngsters on your gift list with twenty or even possibly thirty seconds of enjoyment. We are hoping to see this concept developed further, perhaps ultimately involving a Saturday-morning cartoon show about a family of head lice who have wacky adventures with their friend Toby the Tapeworm.

We might add that the National Pediculosis Association also sells (*really*) a line of lice-related T-shirts. Although we ourselves would be extremely reluctant to put one on.

CRACKER THROWER

$19.50; Orvis, Historic Route 7A, P.O. Box 798, Manchester, Vt. 05254-0798; phone 800-541-3541; Suggested by Carol Bellinger of Spokane, Wash.

This is the perfect gift for anybody on your gift list who has a need for a mechanical device capable of throwing round crackers great distances. According to the Orvis catalogue, this device was designed "to launch crackers into the air as challenging, biodegradable targets for trap shooters." But the catalogue notes that you can also use it "at the beach as a seagull feeder."

The catalogue states that this device, which comes in both right-handed and left-handed models, is capable of throwing a cracker "up to 60 yards at incredible speeds." This leads us to think of a couple of additional uses for it, such as:

PERSONAL PROTECTION In today's crime-ridden urban environment, you can give no more precious gift to a loved one than the gift of security. And think how secure your loved one would feel if he or she had the Orvis Cracker Thrower, pre-loaded, tucked away in his or her pocket or purse, ready to be pulled out the instant that trouble arises. Your hardened urban criminals are definitely going to have second thoughts about attacking a potential victim who is capable of launching a high-speed cracker at close range, especially if it is one of the techno-logically advanced high-impact assault crackers now available to the general public. ("UH-oh! *Sesame seeds!* Let's get out of here!" "Yeah! Those things really sting!")

DINNER PARTIES A major headache for the modern host or hostess who does not have domestic help is trying to keep an eye on things in the kitchen while at the same time making sure that the guests have plenty to nibble on. Think how convenient it would be for the host or hostess on our gift list if, instead of wasting valuable time walking all the way from the kitchen to the living room to replenish the *hors d'oeuvres* tray, he or she could simply load a cracker—perhaps even with a fairly adhe-sive topping on it—into this device and transport it directly to an appreciative guest at speeds normally associated with air-to-air missiles:

HOSTESS (from the kitchen): Roger, how about one more liver *pâte?*

GUEST: Well, I guess I could eat one more (*ZINNNGGGGGGG*) GACK (*thud*).

OTHER GUESTS (hastily): None for us, thanks!

DOG SWEAT SUIT

$17.98; Harriet Carter, Dept. 43, North Wales, Pa. 19455; phone 215-361-5151

*M*ore and more we are coming to realize that dogs are not just stupid moron animals who go around barking violently at air molecules and sniffing each other's private parts for hours at a time. Thanks to best-selling books such as *The Hidden Life of Dogs*, we are now becoming aware that dogs are, in fact, complex, subtle, and sensitive creatures with deep emotional needs. And their number-one need, scientists now believe, is to wear sweat suits. It is a

known fact that dogs left alone in the wild, with no humans to care for them, will form into highly organized packs and spend hours making sweat suits for each other. Granted, these are primitive garments, many of them lacking elastic, or even basic washing instructions. But still they reveal a powerful instinct that is certainly also present in domesticated dogs. That is why we are certain that your dog would love nothing more than to receive this handsome dog sweat suit. We're also sure that even though your pet cannot say "thank you" in so many words, he or she will find some way to express his or her gratitude to you. ("Hey, Mom! Rex pooped in his sweat suit again!")

DOG LIFE VEST

Prices vary from $14.95 to $19.95; The Safety Zone, 2515 E. 43rd St., Chattanooga, Tenn. 37422-7247; phone 800-999-3030. Suggested by George Mundstock of Miami, Fla.

*a*sk yourself this question: How often do you pick up the morning newspaper, read a story about yet another tragic drowning incident involving a dog, then slam your fist down and say: "Can nothing be done to STOP this?"

If you answered, "Four or five times per week, at minimum," then you simply MUST purchase this dog life vest, both for yourself and for the dog-owners on your list.

Perhaps you are saying: "Wait a minute. Don't dogs know how to swim?"

Yes, they know. *Theoretically*. But dogs know a LOT of things, theoretically. We happen to have two dogs, and they *theoretically* know that they are not allowed to eat food off the coffee table.

Nevertheless, there have been a number of times when, having left the living room on a brief errand, we have returned to discover large sectors of pizza missing, and both of our dogs looking guilty and desperately pressing their bodies into the floor, hoping that we will not notice them, or mistake them for large collar-wearing dustballs.

Yes, dogs are fully capable of forgetting the things that they theoretically know, and swimming could be one of these things. We feel that NO dog, in a so-called civilized society, should be allowed to go anywhere NEAR a body of water (including toilets, if it is a small dog) without wearing a life vest. We also think that the federal government should consider requiring that all dogs wear crash helmets. Our larger dog, Earnest, while in pursuit of real or imaginary woodland creatures, routinely runs headfirst into large inanimate objects such as our house. This could theoretically result in damage to her brain, if she had one.

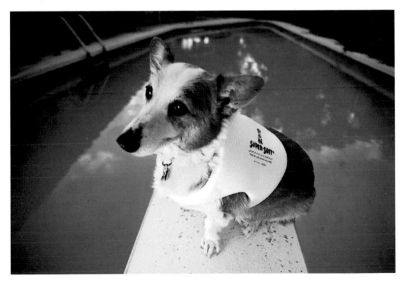

FIGURE-FORMING BRIEF

*W*e cannot think of a nicer way for you to send that Special Someone on your gift list the following message: "You have a really flat butt."

For far too long, few options have been available to buttocks-impaired individuals. Yes, they can do what thousands of top models such as Cindy Crawford do, namely, stuff wads of newspaper down the back of their underwear to achieve a fuller look. Unfortunately, however,

$9.95; Carol Wright Gifts, 340 Applecreek Rd., Lincoln, Neb. 68544-8503; phone 402-474-5174

newspaper ink tends to rub off, which can lead to embarrass-
ment during intimate moments ("Darling, it's not that I don't
find it attractive, but how come you have a picture of Ziggy on
your behind?").

We can kiss this problem good-bye, however, thanks to this
exciting new advance in buttocks enhancement. Not only do
these briefs enable the wearer to LOOK good, but they also
provide vital protection to those unfortunate individuals—and
there are over 17 million of them, according to U.S. Labor
Department statistics—whose jobs require them, for one reason
or another, to sit on thumbtacks.

You will undoubtedly want to purchase a set of these briefs for
every fashion-conscious person on your list—female OR male.

(We understand that Don Shula has fourteen pairs.)

MR. BLINKER COCKTAIL LIGHTS

$1.75 per set of two, batteries not included; American Science & Surplus, 3605 Howard St., Skokie, Ill. 60076; phone 708-982-0870

Technology is constantly improving our lives. Look at the cellular telephone. Just ten years ago, virtually nobody was able to get into a car crash caused by trying to steer and dial at the same time; today, people do this all the time.

Yet there are still certain areas of our life-styles in which, due to a lack of technological advancement, we are still "back in the Stone Age." One such life-style area is the way we order drink refills. For millions of years now, personkind has been using the same old labor-intensive, time-consuming, and often grueling method of lifting a finger at our waitperson or bartender. Many evenings we ourselves have been forced to perform this grueling act repeatedly, and the intense physical effort involved has left us feeling really awful the next morning. Sometimes even our *head* hurts.

That is why we are so thrilled about this gift item, which is featured in the American Science & Surplus catalogue. This is a little battery-powered light with a pocket clip on it. The catalogue states: "It was designed to be hung on your glass in a dark bar to signal when you want a refill. This is not a joke!! That's what it's for!!"

You can just imagine how suave a person would look, clipping a blinking light onto his or her empty drink glass. This would be the ideal gift for the foreign traveler who goes to elegant restaurants in places such as Paris, France, where it is always a good idea to impress the staff with your suaveness and sophistication (*"Garcon!* Mr. Blinker is on! Fill 'er up!").

DOGGIE BAG

$24.95; Collar Craft, P.O. Box 490, Mt. Vernon, Mo. 65712; phone 800-231-0479. Suggested by Mary McDonough of Columbia, S.C.

*D*o you know what's wrong with small dogs?

Well, yes, they DO have the intelligence of chewing gum and a tendency to express their love by peeing on your feet. But that is not what we are getting at. We are getting at the fact that small dogs, because of a foolish design oversight on the part of Mother Nature, do not have handles. Thus you generally have to carry them with both hands, which means that you do not have a hand free to carry, for example, a briefcase. This is why so many small-dog owners are unable to take their dogs with them to work.

And that is why you will want to give this item to the dog-owner on your gift list. This item is basically a nylon harness with a handle; it instantly converts an ordinary small dog into a small dog that can easily be carried anywhere, not just to the office, but also to restaurants, health clubs,

theaters, weddings, bar mitzvahs, and funerals. You need *never again* be without your dog. You can take your dog *everywhere*—just like your cellular phone! In addition to constant companionship, a portable dog can be a powerful deterrent to hardened urban street criminals:

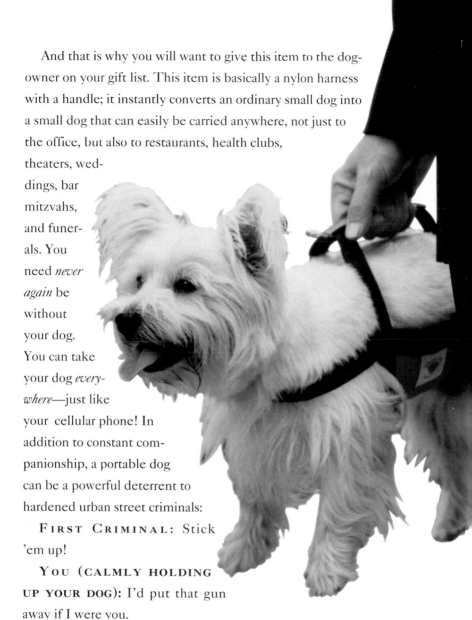

FIRST CRIMINAL: Stick 'em up!

YOU (CALMLY HOLDING UP YOUR DOG): I'd put that gun away if I were you.

SECOND CRIMINAL: Look out, Earl! It's peeing on your feet!

FIRST CRIMINAL: Yikes! Let's get out of here!

NOSE SPREADER

$16 (small), $18 (medium), $21 (large); Robert Sullivan, 3127 Kentwood Dr., Eugene, Ore. 97401; phone 503-686-6650. Suggested by Carol Tomashek of Eugene, Ore.

There is an old saying in the gift-giving business: "Good things come in small packages that you remove the things from and then stick them up your nose." That could not be more true of this item, the Sully Nose Spreader.

This is a real item conceived of and manufactured by a retired engineer, businessman, and inventor, Robert "Sully" Sullivan of Eugene,

Oregon. The Sully Nose Spreader is a device for people who have trouble sleeping because their nose closes up when they lie down to go to sleep (this is known as "nose collapse"). Mr. Sullivan's press release states:

"The spreader is made of chrome steel, the same material used for braces to straighten teeth. Medically safe. To use this spreader, just before you go to bed, insert it into your nose. Go to bed and go to sleep, there is no feeling after you insert the spreader in your nose."

When we ordered the official Gift Guide Nose Spreader from Mr. Sullivan, he sent it with a hand-written letter recounting the following inspirational anecdote:

"One sixty-some-year-old woman came to my home and asked me if I could help her (she lives in England). I told her I would try, she came in and told me she had not breathed through her nose in twenty-five years . . . She put one in her nose and she could breathe. (Through her nose.)"

We actually inserted our Nose Spreader into our personal nose, and we must say that we have never before experienced this degree of comfort with a wire thing up our nose, once we overcame the momentary terror that we would need surgical help to get it back out. Based on this experience, we strongly recommend this item as the ideal gift for anybody on your gift list who needs to breathe. But please make sure that the recipient reads the directions before attempting to use this device. ("No, no, NO! You were supposed to insert it into your NOSE!")